Speed Reading

The Comprehensive Manual Detailing Optimal Strategies
For Enhancing Reading Speed, Comprehension, Memory
Retention, And Cognitive Processing To Foster Superior
Understanding

Artemka Evseeva

TABLE OF CONTENT

How Many Wpm Do You Read?....................................1
Considering The Context...27
Where Do You Stand?..41
"Saccadic Movements, Fixational Paus...............63
The Best Way To Speed Read..................................86
Speed Reading Techniques 111
Mitigate Sub-Vocalization And Minimize Your Eye Movements.. 135

How Many Wpm Do You Read?

It is advisable to select a book that is easily comprehensible and of moderate complexity when undertaking the endeavor of learning to read at an accelerated pace. Novels and children's books of a lighter nature are exceptional choices. A deep knowledge of specific books facilitates a smooth and rapid transition to the practice of speed reading. Steer clear of books that extensively employ unfamiliar jargon, as it can impede your understanding and consequently impede your advancement. Medical texts, physics, and books of similar subject matter should be avoided unless one possesses expertise in these particular fields. Alice's Adventures in Wonderland, To Kill a Mockingbird, and The Diary of a Young Girl are books with which we possess a great degree of familiarity.

These works exemplify a consistent trend of being highly suitable for educational purposes and attaining a high level of accessibility for readers at this juncture.

Exercise

Having made the selection of an appropriate book, please find a tranquil and undisturbed setting in which to engage with its contents. Music is deemed permissible, should it be your preference. Please adjust your timer to one minute and commence reading. Do refrain from attempting to exceed your customary speed. The objective is to achieve a level of reading where you maintain your usual reading speed while comprehending the content fully. Cease reading and delineate your stopping point with a pencil once the timer elapses.

Determining your words per minute (wpm)

To ascertain your words per minute, the initial step entails calculating the mean number of words per line. One can employ a random selection process to choose three lines and proceed to tally the word count for each of those lines. Take, for instance, the scenario when the typical word count per line in paperback novels fluctuates between 8 and 10. In such circumstances, the quantity of words per line would amount to 10. Please ascertain the quantity of lines you have read. In general, it is advisable not to consider a sentence at the end of a paragraph as a full line if it consists of only a few words. Once you have completed the process of verifying the number of lines read, proceed to calculate the result by multiplying it with the total number of words per line. As an illustration, multiplying 23 lines by 10 words per line yields a total of 230 words per minute (wpm).

It is advisable to document both the date and the reading speed in words per minute to monitor and evaluate your improvement.

The Significance of Your Reading Speed

If your reading speed falls within the range of 150 to 400 words per minute, it indicates that you are reading at a pace that is deemed to be within the realm of "typical" or "average." Do not be discouraged if your reading speed is below 150 words per minute. There exist students who have exhibited a reading speed of less than 100 words per minute, but have successfully kept pace with this course, substantially improving their reading speed, ultimately achieving the status of proficient speed readers. Irrespective of one's position along this spectrum, a reading rate falling between 150 and 400 words per minute indicates a comparatively slow pace.

The Fundamental Principles for Achieving Effective Speed Reading

A distinction exists between possessing the knowledge of how to engage in speed reading and one's ability to actively practice it. Academic expertise carries its merit, yet the practical application of theory amidst real-life circumstances presents a distinct challenge. The subsequent content comprises validated strategies for achieving proficiency in speed reading:

- One should never undervalue the significance of maintaining a regular practice routine. You will not achieve your desired outcomes if you engage in sporadic practice. Diligently implementing a well-structured timetable is the foremost prerequisite for achieving accelerated reading proficiency.
- Gradually cultivate your skills without attempting to immediately tackle the advanced level. It is crucial to conduct a realistic assessment of one's reading abilities prior to commencing with the less challenging drills or exercises. The human brain exhibits enhanced learning capabilities through a sequential method, commencing with simpler exercises and progressing towards more challenging ones only upon the successful mastery of preceding stages.

- It is imperative to not disregard the aptitude for understanding. The prevailing belief among individuals is that speed reading primarily involves the act of reading at a rapid pace. Consistently prioritize both the velocity and the comprehension of the concept. The ultimate objective does not lie in rapidly perusing words. The primary goal is to comprehend the text efficiently during rapid reading.
- It is strongly advised against engaging in rapid reading of legal documents, confidential information, terms and policies, agreements, undertakings, and other similar materials. It is preferable to meticulously peruse the text, employing sub-vocalization techniques to read each word individually. It is important to remember to thoroughly review such documents on at least two separate occasions.
- It is imperative to consistently document your reading velocity. By adopting this approach, you will have the means to monitor the progress of your reading ability as you transition

between each level throughout the practice session.

In the subsequent chapter, we shall examine the fundamental speed reading techniques that individuals should employ in order to attain proficiency in speed reading.

Stages of Reading
Cease Sub-Vocalization: Desist Engaging in Self-Conversation
To cease sub-vocalization, it is recommended to engage in gum-chewing or to commence humming a preferred melody, either a personal favorite or one that has been played repeatedly over an extended duration. This enables you to engage your muscles and prevents the repetition of words. In the event that you possess the inclination to articulate words silently while reading, it is possible to place a finger in contact with your lips.
Conceal the words that you have previously perused.

One may utilize an index card to immediately conceal words upon reading them. This will prevent you from revisiting the content you have just read and assist you in avoiding any undue prolongation.

Develop the ability to minimize eye movement.

Frequently, the primary cause of time being squandered during reading is attributed to the restlessness of one's eyes. To mitigate this, it is suggested to employ an index card technique wherein the card is positioned before a line of text and an X mark is promptly made above the initial word.

Subsequently, inscribe another X in alignment with the preceding mark, and subsequently arrange the cards at regular intervals of three words to quickly browse through the primary topics. It is advisable to continue making Xs with consistent spacing until you reach the final word of the line. Attempt to read with rapidity and agility across the index card, while concurrently directing your gaze immediately beneath the mark denoted as X.

Strive to Sustain a Velocity Beyond Your Comprehension

Here, it would be useful to have any tools such as a pencil or pointer that can assist in navigating the text. Progress the guide along the passage whilst enunciating 'one one thousand' in a composed manner and conclude precisely when reaching the end of the line.

It is advised that you allocate a minimum of two minutes to acquaint yourself with the rhythm of the pencil. It is permissible if you experience difficulty in understanding and comprehending any content, as the sole requirement is to maintain concentration on the text and continually move your gaze for a duration of two minutes. Take a brief intermission of two units of time, and subsequently increase the pace.

Progress while rapidly scanning the text. It is advisable to gain at least a rudimentary comprehension of the text in order to proceed.

Peruse the Subject Matter"
"Comprehend the Substance of the Topic
It is imperative that you ensure you acquaint yourself with the content of whatever material you are perusing. This will facilitate your comprehension and handling of the concepts more effectively.

Ensure the Coherence of the Topic in Every Paragraph

Having familiarity with the content of each paragraph will facilitate more efficient and comprehensive navigation of the text. Frequently, the initial sentence functions as the topic sentence, elucidating the central theme or subject matter of the narrative.

Monitor Your Reading Progress by Timing Yourself

Whilst engaging in the act of reading, it is advisable to monitor and regulate the pace at which one progresses. Utilize digital counters available on virtual platforms, or employ quantitative measures such as page counts or the multiplication of words per line with the total number of lines present on the page.

Attempt to establish a time limit of ten minutes, subsequently documenting the extent of reading material covered within that allocated period. Calculate the product of the number of pages and the number of words per page, then divide the result by ten. This will provide you with your rate of words per minute.

Maintain Goals

Practice makes perfect. With consistent practice in reading, you can progressively ascend the different tiers that are determined by the number of words read per minute. Commencing at the age of 12, individuals typically achieve a reading speed of 200-250 words per minute. This rate increases to approximately 300 words per minute for college students, and reaches around 450 words per minute for individuals skilled in the art of skimming texts. Furthermore, advanced readers can comfortably read at speeds of 600-700 words per minute, while professional readers have been known to achieve an impressive rate of 1000 words per minute.

The majority of individuals are able to comprehend 75% of information presented at a rate of 450 words per minute. However, when the speed of presentation increases to 1000 words per minute, the average human's ability to retain information declines. Practitioners of advanced reading employ rigorous methods to achieve this level.

Now that you have acquainted yourself with the advantages of speed-reading, it is now appropriate to delve into the methods that will aid you in cultivating remarkable reading capabilities.

Psychological Readiness in the Art of Rapid Reading

The mind assumes a critical role in facilitating the advancement of speed reading competencies, and by comprehending the functioning of the brain, individuals can expedite the attainment of their intended outcomes, effectively and expeditiously. Each day, our minds are inundated with copious amounts of information that we listen to, read, or even watch. Without adequate mental preparation, harnessing the capabilities of the brain to achieve a high reading speed can present a formidable endeavor. The brain possesses cognitive mechanisms that aid in discerning and selectively attending to information that appears to captivate the reader, continually heightening the reader's awareness of said information throughout the reading experience.

There exists a cerebral region commonly referred to as the reticular activating system, which serves the function of allowing individuals to discern the significance of information presented to them in situations involving a substantial volume of data. As you may be aware, we are frequently inundated with an overwhelming amount of information on a continual basis. Our brains perform the essential function of sifting through and modifying this information, allowing only the most essential elements to capture our attention. Suppose, hypothetically, that you are in the process of studying for an examination and there happen to be particular subjects which pique your interest, warranting your attention.

When you dedicate time to reading, even though you encounter a multitude of information, the majority of what you read undergoes a process of filtering and distortion. However, your reticular activating system will subsequently alert you whenever a word or phrase that pertains to your area of interest is recognized. Consequently, the reticular activating system operates by directing your attention towards the words or phrases that pique your interest.

The conventional method of reading entails the sequential movement of the eyes from left to right, as they consistently scan the paragraph for significant words or phrases that merit contemplation and retention. Once the eyes acclimate to the sequential nature of reading and identify an optimal point of recognition within a sentence, the brain initiates the task of ascribing meaning and interpreting the individual words.

Memory Principles

In light of the perpetually rising magnitude of information demanding human cognition, individuals must be prepared to cultivate the requisite aptitude and cognitive resilience to sustain concentration, or even progress, amidst the voluminous influx of information. Additionally, the sensation of being overwhelmed could potentially stem from one's mindset or overall demeanor. One must possess a familiarity with fundamental principles concerning memory in order to optimize speed reading abilities.

It is crucial to acknowledge that the process of memory is contingent upon factors such as perception, reasoning, and attention, and does not operate in isolation.

Memory cannot be applied to discrete facts alone, as every recollection is intricately intertwined with various pieces of information stored within one's memory bank.

The successful acquisition of information is heavily dependent on the establishment of associations. When one's memory system is properly structured, it allows for efficient retrieval of information.

The new information that is obtained does not exist in isolation from prior memories, as the existing knowledge aids in the understanding and assimilation of the new information, and vice versa. Consequently, this facilitates the reading and comprehension of information that is already familiar to you.

Memory is not only designed for storing information but also for use. It is essential to recognize that memory is not an object, but rather a sequence of cognitive processes occurring continuously within the confines of the human brain.

The capacity of memory, akin to that of other somatic muscles, can be enhanced through dedicated training, resulting in improved information retention and cognitive functionality. In order to become an excellent reader, it is necessary to cultivate one's memory to a level that facilitates efficient information retention and sustained focus, even in situations characterized by an overwhelming abundance of information.

With increased participation in memory training and active utilization, one's memory grows in strength. Some potential factors that contribute to impaired memory function could possibly include inadequate nutrition, insufficient physical activity, ineffective stress management techniques, and excessive physical exertion.

In order to adequately equip oneself for speed reading, it is imperative to possess a comprehensive grasp of three distinct forms of memory: short-term memory, long-term memory, and sensory memory.

1. Sensory Memory

This constitutes the primary manifestation of memory, derived from the five sensory faculties encompassing visual perception, tactile sensitivity, gustatory perception, olfactory perception, and auditory perception. All of these factors contribute to the formation of a sensory memory that is retained by the brain for a brief duration. While it is true that sensory-based memories have a limited duration of a few seconds, it is possible to enhance one's attentiveness in order to facilitate memory enhancement.

This can be achieved by eliciting the activation of the sensory memory during the process of reading. An instance of this can be seen while engrossed in reading a literary work, wherein one can also devote careful observation to the pigmentation of the book's cover, as well as the pictorial representations incorporated within its pages. One can engage the olfactory senses by directing attention towards the surrounding scents, regardless of the setting - be it a library, a residence, or an outdoor location. Subsequently, you can establish a connection between those experiences and the information you are perusing, leading to the realization that recollecting the olfactory impressions of the surroundings enables the retention of the associated knowledge, just as recalling the chromatic characteristics of the book facilitates the remembrance of the information at hand.

2. Short Term Memory

This form of memory pertains to retaining information that is intended for immediate use, such as solving a mathematical problem or responding to an inquiry. The information stored in short-term memory is consequential in the moment and possesses a limited duration of relevance. If you lacked this particular ability, the consequence would be that each and every perception received through the senses would be retained in memory, rendering it easily recollected and available, resulting in an overwhelming cognitive burden.

If one desires to preserve certain information residing in their short-term memory, it is advisable to allocate adequate attention and concentration to the matter at hand.

3. Long-term Memory

This encompasses data that is stored within the cognitive faculties and can be accessible for recall subsequent to a prolonged duration. Repetition facilitates the transfer of information from transient short-term memory to enduring long-term memory. When engaging in the act of reading, it is imperative to employ a certain degree of repetition, as this facilitates the retention of information in the brain over an extended duration. Naturally, the act of repeating information does not necessarily entail reading it multiple times for the purpose of memorization; as a matter of fact, reading it once may suffice for effective retention.

How the memory works

The memory system is affected by cognitive frameworks known as mental models. The memory system can be classified into three distinct categories.

Acquisition, encompassing assimilation of the information being perused

Retention pertains to the process of memorizing and mentally storing the information that has been read.

Information retrieval – Extracting stored data for utilization.

The stored memory may potentially become inaccessible at any given moment, yet this realization only occurs when one attempts to access the information. Suppose you encounter an individual whom you had previously met and were acquainted with their name. As you approach the person again, just before greeting them, you find yourself attempting to recall their name, but curiously it fails to recollect in your memory. Through gaining knowledge about the workings of memory and engaging in memory-enhancing exercises, one can enhance their ability to retain and recall information more effectively.

Here are a few fundamental guidelines you can adhere to in order to enhance your capacity for memory retention:

1. Memory Acquisition

Focusing: The initial action to enhance your capacity for memory acquisition and retention of information involves directing your attention towards the task at hand. On numerous occasions, we inadvertently overlook significant matters due to our initial lack of attentiveness. It is conceivable that one may complete the reading of a book, only to promptly forget its title merely due to insufficient attention paid during the reading process. When experiencing mental preoccupations while reading, the potential outcome is that the retention of the information read may be hindered upon completion of the text.

Strategy: Avoid simply indiscriminately opening a book and commencing the act of reading without a clear purpose. Devote ample time to meticulous planning and ensure you develop a well-defined strategy for incorporating the information gleaned from the book into your intentions. Ensure that your intention or objective for reading is unequivocally established right from the outset. It would be beneficial to demonstrate a degree of curiosity and engagement with the content you are perusing. It might be impracticable to assimilate all the information that you may lack interest in, and the act of retaining such information could pose challenges.

Engage in Active Reading: By failing to actively participate in the reading process, there is a greater likelihood of becoming inadvertently drowsy. Engaging in active reading allows for the integration of existing knowledge with new information, ultimately augmenting one's level of comprehension.

2. Memory Retention

Maintaining knowledge within one's memory is distinct from the ability to recall it whenever needed. Efficient utilization of memory is achieved through effective organization and association, whereby enhancing the capacity to retain and retrieve information promptly and suitably whenever the need arises. There exist various instruments that can be employed to effectively arrange information, thus facilitating its retention and retrieval.

Practice and Review: To improve the retention of information, it is imperative to engage in repeated practice and thorough review of the material set to be memorized. Increased time dedicated to reviewing and practicing the content one has read corresponds to a higher likelihood of effectively retaining it within one's memory.

Considering The Context

As aforementioned, it is noteworthy that the statements uttered by an individual may not warrant primary attention, particularly when one is engaged in the practice of swiftly comprehending the speaker's underlying message. Previously, we deliberated on how the utterances of an individual can possess varying connotations depending on their precise delivery and emphasized the significance of actively attending to more than mere verbal content. Next, we will delve into the topic of context.

Context encompasses the entirety of the situational backdrop, encompassing factors such as the immediate environment, the background and experiences of the interlocutor, and any pertinent particulars that may influence the significance conveyed by the spoken words.

Regarding the topic of speed reading, the significance of context cannot be overstated. As a demonstration, suppose an individual expresses an extraordinary fondness for their occupation while in the presence of their supervisor. In such circumstances, one could infer that their statements might conceivably be embellished or even deliberately fabricated to make a favorable impression on their superior. If an individual expresses their profound admiration for their job when they are in an exclusive setting and you bear no connection to their professional pursuits, it is reasonable to infer that they possess a deep affection for their job.

Not only can context change the meaning of what someone is saying but it can also help you read between the lines. In the preceding illustration, I alluded to the scenario where an individual might express fervent admiration for their occupation while being in close proximity to their supervisor, thereby raising skepticism regarding the veracity of their assertion. Additional contextual information in this particular situation would facilitate the interpretation of implicit messages conveyed by this individual. For illustrative purposes, assume that this individual has previously informed you that their supervisor has been exceptionally demanding and is reputed for disciplining subordinates over minor transgressions. Perhaps you have also observed the discernible frown etched upon the countenance of their superior, concurrently witnessed by the employee displaying a sudden tensing of their posture in response to the presence of their boss. Upon careful observation of the complete picture, this contextual analysis affords you the opportunity to discern a substantially altered underlying message within the employee's words: I feel compelled to express my admiration for my occupation since any criticism, be it related to the job itself or my superior, would likely result in negative consequences.

Although the employee may not be explicitly expressing this message, the context and adeptness of the listener strongly imply that such a message is indirectly implied. One should exercise caution when making substantial inferences about the implication behind someone's words, however, by considering the context and one's initial interpretation, one can gain a reasonable understanding of the underlying message being conveyed.

Let us consider the factors that warrant your attention as you investigate the contextual framework within which a conversation takes place. The initial aspect that we shall delve into pertains to the substance of the discourse.

Occasionally, the semantic implications of an individual's utterances may vary based on the context and content of the preceding discourse. For instance, in the event that a collective of individuals engages in a discourse regarding their challenging work experiences, and an additional individual approaches to join the conversation, it is plausible that this individual too would express that they encountered a difficult day at work. It is possible that they have had a challenging day, but if their overall demeanor appeared upbeat prior to participating in this conversation, it is plausible that they are making such statements to foster a sense of camaraderie within their social circle.

An additional illustration could involve the discussion of statistical data regarding the annual incidence of pit bull attacks. In the event that such a statement is uttered within a dialogue focused on the adoration of all dog breeds or in the presence of a gathering comprised of individuals who harbor affection for pit bulls, it is possible that the intention behind the remark is to imply that the quantity referenced is exceedingly minute. Should they express such sentiment in their capacity as exclusive owners of golden retrievers, whilst they traverse a barking pit bull, it is plausible that their intention resides in deeming this magnitude as excessive and disconcerting.

It is evident that the substance of a dialogue possesses the capacity to notably influence the significance conveyed by an individual's expressions.

The significance of an individual's words can also be influenced by their actions. If an individual engages in their daily morning run and admits to making unhealthy dietary choices the previous evening, their perspective likely differs significantly from someone who habitually orders take-out and watches Netflix in their living room every evening.

An additional factor that can impact the setting of a discourse is individual behavior. Should an individual possess the inclination to continuously exhibit an exaggerated level of enthusiasm in all their utterances, even for trivial matters, it is plausible that they may display an excessively joyous demeanor upon realizing a mere three-cent reduction in the price of gasoline per gallon compared to the previous day. In the absence of familiarity with this individual, one might presume that their exuberance stems from discovering prospects to preserve nominal sums of money. Should you be acquainted with said individual, you would undoubtedly be aware that their narrative is not genuinely as captivating as it appears, for they tend to passionately recount most of the occurrences in their life.

An additional factor pertaining to the dynamics of conversation that warrants discussion is the influence of behavioral patterns. As an illustration, if an individual acquaints you with their involvement in a physical altercation at a drinking establishment on the preceding evening, you may express apprehension regarding their well-being and possibly even their psychological state. It may be advisable to make an effort to aid them in overcoming their challenges. If you possess a strong familiarity with the individual and are aware that such incidents occur on a routine basis, your response may not be driven by astonishment or empathy.

The disparity between an individual expressing veracity and an individual engaging in deceit can significantly impact the overall context of a discourse. Certainly, if one possesses the knowledge that the individual with whom they engage in conversation is being deceitful, it becomes evident that placing trust in any information conveyed by said person is ill-advised. Furthermore, you possess knowledge of their ulterior motive for deceiving, thus enabling you to employ your adept speed-reading skills to discern the true nature of said motivation. When employing speed-reading techniques to discern a person's veracity, one's comprehension of the conversation's context and the intended connotations of its words undergoes a substantial shift.

Another factor that can impact the context in which an individual's words are interpreted is their thought process. In the event that an individual's thoughts are directed towards an entirely separate matter from the ongoing conversation, their verbal expressions may potentially deviate from their actual thoughts, resulting in a lack of intrinsic significance. If an individual exhibits thoughtful consideration in their speech, it indicates a genuine commitment to expressing their true intentions and a vested interest in the subject matter at hand.

The context of a situation may also be influenced by the emotional state of individuals. In the event that an individual is in a heightened state of distress or harboring intense feelings of anger towards you, it is possible for them to utter statements that do not align with their true intentions. If they exhibit emotional equilibrium, their statements can be placed under greater trust.

The subjective motive of an individual can indeed exert an impact on the context of a conversation, consequently influencing the intended significance behind their words. Take, for instance, when individuals engage in a job interview, their ultimate objective is to secure employment. They may engage in verbal misrepresentation or fabrication, aiming to create a favorable impression on the interviewer.

The integrity of the individual who is speaking can also influence the circumstances surrounding a conversation. If one is aware of their reputation for upholding strong moral principles, it is reasonable to infer that their statements are truthful. In the event that their integrity is questionable, it would be advisable to observe their non-verbal cues, as they may provide insight into the veracity of their statements.

In conclusion, one's work habits can impact the circumstances surrounding a conversation. In the event that an individual is characterized as industrious, for instance, and they express that their day was challenging, it can be inferred that their assertion is most likely accurate. If they exhibit a proclivity for idleness, it may be prudent to exercise some caution in regarding their credibility.

In general, it becomes evident that the context has the potential to significantly impact a conversation and the interpretation of words. Allow us to engage in an exercise to facilitate the development of your contextual skills.

In the following examples, devise alternative approaches whereby the contextual framework may potentially influence the connotation and interpretation of the given terms. Feel free to exercise your creativity to the fullest extent.

I exerted a considerable amount of effort today. I require a moment of respite at present."

We extend our warm invitation to join us for dinner this evening, should you wish to do so.

"I love my job. I aspire to endure it indefinitely.

"If I didn't live so far away, I am sure that we would hang out way more often."

Maintaining chameleons as domesticated animals can pose challenges. It is imperative for potential buyers to possess a deeper understanding of these animals prior to making a purchase."

The cleanliness of my residence is truly exceptional today!

Where Do You Stand?

What is the significance of your words per minute (wpm) score?

Undoubtedly, you aspire to enhance your reading speed by a factor of four upon completing this book and through consistent practice. However, it should be noted that there exist objective benchmarks that indicate the attainment of speed reading proficiency. These observations are noteworthy, as they enable you to ascertain your present status and envision your desired future state through diligent practice.

Outlined below are the frequently utilized speed classifications for readers. Please take the time to ascertain which level you currently fall into and make a mental observation regarding your desired proficiency. This will serve as a positive source of motivation for you going forward.

- 1 – 200 words per minute: This reading speed is indicative of vocalization during the reading process, wherein the reader articulates the words aloud at a similar pace as their natural speech tempo. Further elucidation regarding the ramifications of vocalization will be expounded upon in subsequent chapters. However, it should be acknowledged that maintaining a consistent pace between speaking and learning necessitates limitations to reading speed, thereby necessitating a cessation of such a practice.

- At a rate of 200 – 300 words per minute, your reading speed aligns with the average comprehension level of individuals, taking into account that the average individual does not actively pursue learning as a personal interest.

This indicates that you possess a certain degree of familiarity with the content you are reading, although your infrequent reading habit leads to the tendency of vocalizing the text, consequently impeding your reading speed.

• Readers falling within the range of 300 – 700 words per minute: This particular group, often regarded as demonstrating above-average skills, tend to process words in clusters and are likely to incorporate reading as an integral part of their everyday routines. In this instance, there is a restriction on the use of oral communication, albeit accompanied by a broad range of linguistic expressions, in order to facilitate the enhanced capacity for rapid reading and comprehension.

At a reading rate of 700 words per minute, you are displaying indications of possessing the skills of a proficient speed reader. It is likely that you have incorporated certain principles of speed reading into your reading habits and have become proficient in their application. Without exception, it is desirable to maintain a rate of words per minute within this range. However, the particular numerical objective you establish for yourself relies on your initial reading pace prior to engaging in speed reading exercises.

When commencing a training regimen (for the purpose of weight loss, bodybuilding, or any other objective), the initial step undertaken by your trainer will be to evaluate your current status and ascertain your present physical condition. This principle applies similarly to the practice of speed reading. Prioritize the assessment of your current reading speed as a crucial step towards gauging your abilities and setting a tangible target for improvement.

Methods to Enhance the Rate of Absorption

Having improved your peripheral vision, the subsequent task is to augment the speed at which you cognize information. The subsequent suggestions will prove to be useful.

Focus

To attain proficiency in reading, one must possess unwavering concentration. It is evident that should your attention be preoccupied, you will inevitably struggle to comprehend the material at hand. As previously mentioned, employing a tool to monitor and measure your pace can prove to be advantageous. Being situated in an appropriate setting can also contribute to minimizing distractions.

Engage in reading for concepts rather than focusing solely on the literal words.

The concept underlying the act of reading is to communicate concepts and significance. Certain words are more pertinent than others. For example, words such as "to, by, of, and, the" and similar ones are comparatively inconsequential, thus it is possible to efficaciously omit them without any loss of significance. In the following sentence:

The young lady proceeded to purchase ice cream from the grocery store.

By perusing the text entitled "girl went ice cream grocery," all pertinent information may be acquired.

Take breaks

There is typically a point at which one encounters challenges in maintaining concentration and comprehension. You begin to observe a decrease in your reading speed, which serves as a remarkable illustration of the concept of diminishing returns in the field of economics. In the event that this occurrence transpires, kindly set aside the book momentarily and avail yourself of a brief respite. Permit yourself to engage in occasional online research, engage in a game of fetch with your canine companion, perform a few sets of calisthenics, or procure a cup of coffee or water. After the conclusion of the intermission, resume your literary pursuits with revitalized vigor.

Practice speed drills

This exercise can be characterized as a preliminary practice, specifically designed to enhance the functioning of your visual perception. There is no need for concern with regard to understanding the information. The objective is to effectively familiarize your brain and eyes with advanced reading velocities. Determine the duration required for you to complete the reading of a single page in a book, and subsequently endeavor to accomplish the reading of an additional page within half of that time. Do this five times. An alternative approach would be to utilize web-based resources such as Readfa.st or Accelereader, where you can adjust the reading speed to 1.5 times or double your typical rate.

How to Enhance Cognitive Capacity for Reading Comprehension

Irrespective of the rate at which your visual perception processes textual information, it is imperative to possess the capacity to ascertain the intended significance behind the words. The subsequent recommendations can facilitate an enhancement in your brain's cognitive capacities to increase your rate of comprehension:

Pre-read the text

Prior to embarking on the comprehensive reading of a book, it is prudent to mentally prime oneself for the forthcoming subject matter. Examine the front and back covers, peruse the table of contents, and inspect the inner flaps of the book. In addition to reviewing the headings and subheadings, it would also be advisable to peruse the introductory and concluding paragraphs of each chapter. One notable benefit of engaging in pre-reading material lies in its capacity to prime and acquaint your mind with pertinent information and key areas to be attentively aware of. Analogously, akin to the way in which recording affirmations supports instructing the brain on focal points for the day, pre-reading material assists in guiding cognitive concentration. Engaging in pre-reading activities can provide you with a more comprehensive outlook, enabling you to integrate the specific details as you engage with the material.

Inquire preemptively "

This serves an equivalent purpose as pre-reading. The objective is to mentally prepare one's cognitive faculties to process the forthcoming data by furnishing preliminary facts and situating the text within a relevant framework. There are certain inquiries that you ought to reflect upon, namely: the central concept, the genre of the written work, and the ulterior motive of the author.

Adjust the pace at which you read

A proficient writer effectively conveys the central concept of a given paragraph through the use of a topic sentence. When commencing a new paragraph, it is imperative to diminish your reading pace in order to comprehend the forthcoming content more thoroughly, subsequently accelerating your speed while perusing the accompanying information.

Take notes

Attempt to condense each paragraph into a solitary term or concept, and subsequently record it on the margins, or employ a mind map to visually annotate. Conduct a comprehensive examination subsequent to your completion of the reading material, wherein you revisit the table of contents and scrutinize the concepts presented in each respective section.

Discuss with others

If you genuinely wish to ascertain your comprehension of the subject matter, engage in discussions with individuals to exchange knowledge and perspectives. One can accomplish this by, for example, establishing or becoming a member of a literary society. Alternatively, you have the opportunity to impart your acquired knowledge onto another individual.

Refining Your Purpose: A Guide to Specificity

Commence perusing in an effortless manner.

Establishing a purpose in your reading constitutes the foremost imperative. Failure to do so results in aimless drifting and the squandering of significant amounts of time.

An explicitly articulated objective serves as the foundation of all endeavors.

As a case in point, consider the methodology employed to achieve the momentous feat of landing a human being on the lunar surface in the year 1969. How were we able to accomplish it? Have we recently embarked on the construction of a spacecraft, wherein we have placed individuals in the capsule and dispatched them into outer space with a casual, dismissive farewell? Furthermore, after reaching outer space, one of them has conceived an idea and proposed, "Dear colleagues, I am experiencing some stiffness in my legs. Would it not be amenable for us to redirect this vessel towards the moon so that we may partake in a leisurely stroll?"

Nope. The event did not unfold in the manner described. NASA approached the task systematically, carefully delineating each stage with clear objectives to be achieved. Each time they launched an object or individual into space, they did so with a distinct and precise objective in mind. Do you recall the Apollo program, by any chance?

Apollo 7

October 11, 1968. Dispatch the inaugural manned Apollo mission to outer space. Meeting with Saturn IVB was a success. A total of 163 rotations around the Earth.

Apollo 8

December 21, 1968. Dispatch a trio of individuals aboard the Saturn V spacecraft. Embark on a circumnavigation of the Moon on the evening of December 24th. Communications and tracking demonstrations.

Apollo 9

March 3, 1969. Conduct the inaugural piloted test mission of the Lunar Module. Docking and propulsion demonstrations. Relocate personnel within and outside the vessel. A total of 151 revolutions around the Earth.

Apollo 10

May 18, 1969. Orbit the Moon. Deploy the Lunar Module in close proximity to the lunar surface within a distance of 9 miles. Lunar Module (LM) rendezvous and Command Module (CM) docking within the gravitational field of the moon.

Apollo 11

July 16, 1969. Dispatch Neil Armstrong, Michael Collins, and Edwin "Buzz" Aldrin into space. Successfully achieve lunar landing on July 20. Take core samples. Plant the American flag.

The main objective is as follows:

In the event of being unaware of your intended destination

You shall eventually find yourself in a different location!

In order to optimize your reading experience and ensure that your time invested yields the maximum benefit, it is imperative to approach your reading with a clear and specific objective in mind. Period.

Today is my designated day of rest, during which I plan to immerse myself in the pages of this captivating book, relishing each eloquent depiction it offers with a deliberate and unhurried pace. Speed is of no consequence to me.

I strongly dislike all the materials I encounter at my workplace, including business journals, memos, and reports. E-mails, in particular, evoke a sense of aversion within me. I aim to obtain a comprehensive understanding expeditiously in order to prioritize more significant matters.

I have recently established my own business and I require a website. I have recently made a purchase of a rather substantial book on the subject matter of web design. My aspiration does not revolve around achieving expertise, rather it entails acquiring sufficient knowledge to construct a concise collection of webpages featuring product descriptions, as well as information pertaining to the company and my personal background.

My spouse consistently withdraws from conversations whenever I attempt to address certain matters concerning our relationship, leaving me perplexed as to the underlying cause. I have recently acquired a book that spans 300 pages, titled "How To Preserve Your Marriage."

I am currently seeking an immediate response to the following inquiry: What is the reason behind men's inclination to withdraw?

I am currently pursuing a course in nuclear engineering at the Massachusetts Institute of Technology (MIT), and in a span of four weeks, we will be assessed through a written examination on the subject matter encompassing the Principles of Structural Mechanics. Our educator has addressed the essential components that necessitate our understanding, and we have been instructed to peruse the contents of these three literary works.

While the majority of these purposes encompass a wide range, they facilitate the development of a proper approach towards our reading materials.

Take into consideration the alternative viewpoint and the typical method that the majority of individuals employ when engaging in the act of reading.

Compulsively Read Everything!

Frequently, this approach stems from an initial inclination towards indolence or lethargy in the early stages of projects, wherein we often succumb to the temptation of simply reading all the material without much effort. Moreover, it emanates from a sense of guilt if we fail to read the entire book and a fear of potentially overlooking significant information if we begin to skip portions of it.

Indeed, the notion that one must value each utterance and acquire all information is the initial indication that one should take a moment to articulate their goals. Once you have identified your requirements from the material, you can subsequently employ the appropriate strategies that will enable you to achieve your objective in the most expeditious manner.

Please take note: Failure to read with a clear objective leads to a lack of specificity and haphazardly acquiring information without any guiding purposes. There is a possibility that you may experience confusion and disorganization, and it is probable that you will encounter challenges in retaining the information you read. Alternatively: "Even more troubling is the possibility that you devote valuable efforts to memorizing superfluous information, only to realize its irrelevance when it becomes too late."

Devoting time to determining a precise objective prior to commencing the act of reading yields a multitude of advantageous outcomes.

If the goals, objectives, or purposes resonate with your personal inclinations and capture your interest, you will experience a heightened emotional investment in the process of reading. The formation of strong memories is fundamentally rooted in emotions, thus leading to an enhanced capacity for information retention.

Memory operates in accordance with the principle of association. In other words, preexisting knowledge will serve as foundational elements upon which you can build and integrate new information. When engaging in the formulation of precise inquiries, such as in the meticulous definition of a purpose, it will yield the establishment of initial junctures (anchors) for all incoming information encountered. Remembering will be facilitated as a result of clear delineation, perceptible identification, and interconnectedness.

By determining precisely the requirements and underlying purpose of the material, individuals can cultivate enhanced motivation and concentration, facilitating the successful completion of the task at hand. This tends to stimulate the cognitive process and foster a more assertive attitude towards the subject matter.

"Saccadic Movements, Fixational Paus

Having a comprehension of the way in which our eyes navigate a page during speed reading will significantly impact your reading proficiency. If you have ever had the opportunity to witness someone engage in the practice of speed reading, you are poised to derive great pleasure from the ensuing encounter. They possess the capability to swiftly manipulate the pages of a book at a speed that exceeds the bounds of human imagination. One might assume that they are simply jesting and not paying attention to the material, but in actuality, they possess the ability to recall and reiterate the information acquired from the book once they have completed reading it. Whilst a traditional reader may occasionally struggle to retain the information presented on a page, a speed reader can efficiently complete the task at hand while effectively retaining said information.

It is imperative to note that a crucial factor in enhancing speed reading lies in optimizing the functionality of one's visual faculties. The eyes act as the sensory organs responsible for scanning the page, assimilating information, and subsequently relaying it to the brain. Individuals who have acquired considerable experience in the art of rapid reading do not necessarily possess exceptional intelligence or possess an enigmatic visual acuity. They possess equivalent visual acuity as their peers, having acquired the ability to enhance their reading speed and manipulate their eye movements in a manner conducive to this.

The initial aspect to consider regarding achieving proficiency in speed reading pertains to the ocular structures. In order to effectively comprehend written documents or other textual materials, irrespective of your chosen reading pace, it is essential to possess a strong visual acuity. This necessitates ensuring regular eye examinations. If one possessed exceptional rapid reading abilities in the past, one would inevitably encounter difficulties in maintaining such a pace given any decline in visual acuity.

For an extensive duration, it was commonly held that the acquisition of peripheral vision skills was necessary in order to engage in the practice of speed reading. When discussing peripheral vision, we are alluding to the visual field that we can effectively utilize and observe through the outer edges of our field of view. The concept entailed the notion that the eyes would traverse and examine the page, while the words residing within the periphery would be retained. However, further investigation has revealed that this assertion is unfounded, and in actuality, employing this approach may lead to a significant loss in text comprehension.

Conversely, it is imperative in the practice of speed reading to possess the ability to comprehensively scan the entirety of a given text. This methodology is poised to greatly enhance your ability to comprehensively grasp each word and expression, similar to how one would when employing the strategy of peripheral vision. The significance of your visual faculties in the speed reading process cannot be overstated, as they are instrumental in comprehending and assimilating information. Ensuring their optimal functioning and alignment with your desired pace is imperative. There are certain challenges that may arise when attempting to engage in speed reading, such as commonly encountered obstacles that tend to distract the eyes and hinder the process. We shall dedicate a portion of this chapter to discussing these matters at length, as well as engaging in eye exercises aimed at enhancing the efficacy of speed reading.

The problem pertaining to saccades and ocular functioning

Saccades are equally significant in facilitating an individual's exploration of the external environment and enhancing their reading speed. A saccade refers to a swift and abrupt motion of the eye as it shifts between points of fixation. Therefore, the efficacy of your reading speed is directly proportional to the speed at which you execute these rapid eye movements and the distance between your fixation points.

Occasionally, one may find themselves with limited influence over the occurrence of saccades. As an illustration, in the event that certain words within the text are unfamiliar to you, it is likely that the saccade will encompass a reduced region, resulting in diminished reading speed. Conversely, if you possess a familiarity with the information at hand and a comprehensive understanding of the words articulated, it is likely that your rapid eye movements can be accelerated, resulting in a greater distance between fixations. This will ultimately facilitate an enhancement in your speed.

The majority of individuals will encounter difficulty due to the slowed rate of their rapid eye movement, primarily caused by the close proximity between fixation points. It is possible that they can only accommodate a limited number of rods at once, and although they may execute this swiftly, every instance of pausing the eye movement will significantly impede their speed.

Enhancing Reading Efficiency through Fixations

An additional element of speed reading concerns the phenomenon known as eye fixation. Eye fixation refers to a specific focal point where the eyes naturally settle during the act of reading. Individuals who possess the skill of expediting these fixations are capable of enhancing the quantity of words encompassed within each fixation, consequently leading to an overall increase in reading speed. The quantity of words that can be comprehended during an eye fixation is contingent upon an individual's level of familiarity with the presented material, their personal lexicon, and even the extent of their visual perception.

The broader your visual range, the greater capacity you have to process multiple words simultaneously, consequently enhancing your reading speed when perusing the document. It is imperative to enhance your capacity to assimilate a greater number of words consecutively in order to improve your reading speed. Let us consider the following sentence for examination: 'The precipitation in the region of Spain remains primarily within the flat land.' An ordinary reader may possess a limited visual attention span, necessitating at least six distinct eye fixations to comprehend the aforementioned sentence fully. In fact, some individuals are only capable of processing one or two words at a time. However, in the case that the reader possesses the skill of speed reading, it is conceivable that they could complete this task within a minimal number of eye fixations. In fact, if their proficiency is exceptionally high, they might even accomplish it in a single fixation.

The more extensive your vocabulary, the greater your capacity to effortlessly navigate the text with your eyes. If you encounter numerous unfamiliar words that pose difficulties for you, your natural inclination will be to pause frequently and fixate your attention on those particular words, thereby impeding the overall speed of your reading. Whenever individuals encounter unfamiliar words, they tend to pay greater attention to them. Consequently, expanding one's vocabulary serves as an effective strategy for enhancing reading speed.

Lastly, the extent of your familiarity with the subject matter will influence the quantity of words that can be perceived within a single ocular fixation. When you engage in studying a subject matter that aligns with your extensive knowledge or falls within your area of interest, your reading proficiency is enhanced as you read with greater assurance. Consequently, you are able to comprehend and assimilate the material more effortlessly, requiring fewer moments of gaze fixation due to your familiarity with the information presented, including relevant terminology.

Your personal background, educational background, and overall breadth of knowledge will also exert an influence on the pace at which you can comprehend written material. Individuals possessing a vast breadth and depth of information are likely to exhibit enhanced reading speed due to their habitual engagement in this pursuit. Speed reading promotes the cultivation of pleasurable and highly efficient reading practices, thus fostering a sense of enthusiasm towards learning. Embracing speed reading techniques enables the expansion of one's knowledge base, facilitating continued progress in reading speed.

Is the practice of speed reading truly effective?

In circumstances where you are faced with an extensive volume of materials that demands careful examination, coupled with limited time constraints that impede thorough reading, it is conceivable that an earnest desire may arise for possessing the skill of accelerated reading. In such circumstances, individuals commonly seek out life hacks and alternative methods to optimize their time and effectively navigate these obstacles. There exists a plethora of speed-reading applications and instructional programs in circulation. However, one must inquire as to their true efficacy in assisting individuals.

Indeed, it should be acknowledged that the majority of available resources may not be adequately equipped to assist in the achievement of one's speed-reading objectives. Particularly those that assert their ability to expedite the process with minimal exertion on your part. The notion of speed reading is not a novel idea. It has been present for a considerable duration, and specialists have been enhancing the methodologies in order to augment its efficacy for individuals seeking to acquire knowledge.

Significant advancements have been made in the realm of speed reading since its initial introduction. Furthermore, in recent times, notable technological advancements have greatly contributed to addressing this matter. Utilizing diverse categories of resources that provide assistance will greatly contribute to one's progress. Subsequently, we will additionally delve into several exceptional applications that can aid you in your endeavor to enhance your reading speed.

As per experts in the field of reading, the reading process encompasses two fundamental components: the assimilation of words and the subsequent comprehension or meaningful interpretation thereof. Hence, it can be inferred that claiming to be an adept speed reader is justified only when one is capable of swiftly comprehending the entirety of the material read. In an alternate scenario, irrespective of one's reading speed, the process would lack significance.

Yes, speed reading works. However, attaining the status of a proficient speed reader necessitates acquiring the requisite skills and actively facilitating the learning process. For example, focusing on vocabulary development and actively improving reading comprehension will greatly contribute to your growth as an adept speed reader. Regarding the practice of speed reading, there is no quick and effortless solution. Do not perceive it as a panacea. Rather, consider it as a sequential progression, a proficiency that necessitates continuous learning and honing in order to attain expertise. Indeed, even if you have attained an advanced level of proficiency as a speed reader, it remains crucial to persistently engage in practice and refinement in order to prevent regression of this skill. One could also alter one's perspective in order to derive greater satisfaction from reading seemingly mundane materials.

Comparing Speed Reading to Photo Reading

The sole similarity between speed reading and photo reading lies within the shared element of the activity referred to as "reading." The origins of speed reading can be traced back to the 1940s, with its subsequent rise in popularity being credited to the efforts of Evelyn Wood. Essentially, speed reading entails the same principles as traditional reading, but at an accelerated pace. Instead of proceeding through the text on a word-by-word basis, you engage with it by comprehending phrases, sentences, and paragraphs. Similarly to the act of reading, speed reading is predominantly governed by the left hemisphere of the brain or the realm of conscious awareness.

In contrast, photo reading can be regarded as a comparatively contemporary notion, stemming from research conducted during the 1970s and the 1980s. Nevertheless, the notion of photo reading only materialized within literary works during the 20th century. Photo reading engages the faculties of the right hemisphere or the subconscious cognition. By means of this procedure, individuals acquire the ability to refrain from relying solely on the written words, but rather on the intellectual processes occurring within their minds. Instead of rapidly shifting your gaze, it would be more efficient to utilize your cognitive faculties more effectively.

Speed reading imparts the skill of rapidly assimilating textual material. Subsequently, as your proficiency in speed reading increases, you will gain the capacity to swiftly peruse written content, without compromising your comprehension. As one acquires knowledge, it is imperative to engage in deliberate and repeated exercises of the skill in order to enhance proficiency.

In order to engage in photo reading, it is imperative to induce a state of relaxation commonly referred to as the 'accelerated learning state,' as it enhances one's awareness levels. It is imperative that one permits their mental and physical faculties to unwind, thereby fostering enhanced receptivity to the entirety of the insights conveyed within the material. During the process of photo reading, it is possible to read books at a rapid pace, averaging approximately 25,000 words per minute. However, it is important to note that in the initial stages, comprehension may not be at optimal levels. Higher levels of understanding are attained during the subsequent phase referred to as the "activation" stage. However, the majority of individuals who begin photo reading do not generally exhibit concern regarding comprehension, thereby alleviating any potential stress associated with the process.

Essentially, speed reading pertains to the acquisition of techniques that enable individuals to read and comprehend written material rapidly, whereas photo reading encompasses a broader scope beyond mere speed. Certain individuals argue that this method enables a novel and distinct approach to acquiring knowledge compared to traditional reliance on written material. Certainly, our primary emphasis lies in the realm of speed reading within the context of this particular book. Therefore, should you desire to acquire further knowledge on the topic of photo reading, it would be advisable to conduct independent research pertaining to the matter.

Rapid Reading, Overviewing, and Perusal

Prior to delving further into the concept of 'normal reading' and its various implications on speed reading, it is essential to establish a precise definition. Fundamentally, the act of reading does not encompass the cognitive process of meticulously analyzing written content in order to ascertain the intended significance behind every sentence, phrase, and individual term. Please be mindful that certain forms of literature are intentionally crafted to incorporate varying degrees of ambiguity. Reading is a cognitive endeavor that involves the assimilation of written content followed by cognitive processing aimed at comprehending its intended significance.

Apart from individuals seeking to keep their readers perplexed, the majority of authors strive for their readers to completely grasp the intended message they wish to convey. Additionally, they desire for their readers to comprehend every single word present within the textual content. Typically, individuals engaging with literary works, scholarly articles, instructional manuals, or similar written materials endeavor to acquire new knowledge or insights. Hence, achieving success in reading entails more than mere identification of the sequential arrangement of individual words. Furthermore, it is crucial to comprehend the interconnections among these words and deduce any implicit elements within the depicted scenarios.

One can draw a distinction between reading and skimming by recognizing that the objective of the latter approach is to swiftly peruse the text, allowing one's gaze to swiftly pass over the words in order to locate a particular term, ascertain a specific piece of information, or form a general understanding of the content. As we will delve into later, the speed of skimming can exceed the rates at which individuals silently read at a typical pace by up to fourfold. Moreover, the extent of understanding tends to be diminished when engaging in superficial reading as opposed to thorough reading. This demonstrates the existence of a potential compromise between the velocity at which you process information and the precision of your understanding.

So... Where would speed reading be positioned within the spectrum of reading techniques that ranges from skimming to thorough reading? Indeed, it can be asserted that speed reading does not truly fall within this spectrum.

On the contrary, speed reading encompasses the combined techniques of reading and skimming. By utilizing speed reading techniques, one can efficiently peruse content at a rapid pace while actively striving to comprehend its meaning. Skimming is among the techniques that can be utilized when acquiring the skill of speed reading. Nevertheless, it will necessitate more than a cursory perusal of the text devoid of any attempt to comprehend its contents. Speed reading is an exceptional aptitude that enables individuals to simultaneously utilize their swiftness and understanding to accomplish greater feats.

The Best Way To Speed Read

Acquiring the skill of rapid reading ought not to be perceived as an arduous task. One could initiate this undertaking by demonstrating adaptability and resilience.

Employ Effective Manipulation of Manual Techniques

Develop the agility of your index finger to traverse swiftly beneath lines of text, allowing your eyes to keep pace. Subsequently, expeditiously relocate it to the initial word in the subsequent line. This specific method can serve as a helpful tool for directing your gaze while engaging in rapid reading.

Relax While At It

It is imperative that you acquire the ability to remain calm and focus simultaneously during the practice of speed-reading. Maintaining a state of relaxation enables you to concentrate on processing the content of the words you have read, rather than solely focusing on the speed at which you read. This requires dedication and consistent effort, but with persistence, you will eventually achieve success. It is important to bear in mind that comprehension plays a crucial role in understanding any text. It is advisable not to engage in rapid reading if the content is incomprehensible or difficult to retain.

Eliminating Verbal Communication

Cease deliberating on the concept of the "oral expression." Although you may not articulate the words silently as you peruse, it is probable that you mentally evoke (or subvocalize) the words you previously pronounced audibly. While it may prove advantageous when perusing complex literary works, it will be rendered futile for the purpose of rapid comprehension. Develop the discipline to interrupt yourself whenever such a occurrence arises. If you have a tendency to vocalize while reading, I recommend employing your fingers to gently obstruct your lips until such time as this habit is discontinued.

Consume words in clusters

The essential principle is to refrain from approaching each word in isolation. Simultaneously read and comprehend clusters of words. This enables reduced ocular movement, thereby facilitating enhanced reading speed.

It is beneficial to locate a sufficiently illuminated and tranquil setting.

Reading comprehension may potentially improve even in the presence of background music or amidst the bustling atmosphere of a crowded coffee shop. However, by minimizing such distractions, you will be able to achieve higher levels of reading speed and comprehension. If you are unable to locate a tranquil setting to establish yourself in (reading in bed is not a viable option), you may consider employing earplugs as a means to mitigate the disturbances.

Ensure that you dedicate time to reading while maintaining a state of mental alertness and engagement.

It is an established truth that individuals perform optimally during the morning hours. Several individuals have demonstrated their capacity for more effective cognitive processes in the afternoon. Take a moment to consider your preferred environment, and then commence your reading.

Chapter Six: The Correlation Between Speed-Reading and Comprehension

The ability to read quickly and fully understand the content encompasses the entirety of the concept. Failure to understand the content expeditiously results in non-attainment of any sort. Pay attention to improving your understanding of what you read. To accomplish this, engage in rapid reading during the early hours of the day. This is the optimal environment for utmost concentration and enhanced retention of information as compared to reading at night.

One valuable suggestion to improve your understanding would be to engage in brief periods of out-loud reading. Engaging in a 30 to 40-minute reading session followed by intermittent breaks stimulates cognitive function. The intervals provide an opportunity for you to thoroughly assimilate the information you have just read and concentrate on the subject matter. This can be most effectively accomplished in a tranquil setting that offers minimal disturbances.

In addition, endeavor to observe and assess your progress in understanding. Reflect upon what knowledge and insights you have amassed throughout your journey. In the event that you encounter difficulty responding to the question, we recommend revisiting the pertinent material. Alternatively, you may seek assistance from another individual in order to enhance your comprehension of the subject matter.

Annotate

Engage in active participation by underlining, circling, and making general notes in the margins. It is imperative that you create a personalized guide to facilitate the identification of crucial elements that necessitate additional consideration. This also aligns your actions with the objectives of the content you have just consumed. It is advisable to briefly survey the chapters beforehand by carefully observing the title pages, subtitles, introductions, and chapter summaries prior to thoroughly delving into each chapter.

The Advantages Offered by Skimming

Undoubtedly, skimming exerts a palpable influence on comprehension. It is recommended that you refrain from engaging in superficial reading practices such as skimming when your intention is to fully grasp and comprehend the material you are about to peruse. Skimming is most appropriately employed when conducting research or obtaining the overall concept of the text.

However, given the constraints of limited time, employing a rapid reading technique can facilitate your understanding. In contrast to typical reading, utilizing the technique of skimming can lead to enhanced comprehension of the central concepts contained within full texts, particularly when one allocates sufficient time for thorough perusal.

Conversely, there have been research studies indicating that particular speed-reading programs, which emphasize techniques primarily focused on quickly scanning written material, have yielded unexpectedly diminished levels of comprehension. Critics of the practice of speed-reading held the opinion that engaging in speed-reading equates to skimming rather than genuinely reading the material.

4 LEVELS OF READING

Subsequently, direct your attention towards Mortimer Adler's delineation of the four levels of reading as expounded in his work "How to Read." Firstly, there will be primary level assessments, followed by secondary level evaluations. Number three analytical. Number four Sin topical. The progression of each subsequent step is built upon the foundation of the preceding step. Foundational literacy skills were imparted to you during educational assessment in your schooling. Reading can manifest in two ways. A couple of brief, leisurely perusals. Skimming the books preface. The genuine process of effective comprehension commences in the Table of Contents index and inside jacket, particularly through the engagement of analytical reading and topical reading with analytical reading. You exhibit a more comprehensive approach to reading books, surpassing even your own previous standards. In accordance with four guiding principles designed to assist in contextual comprehension of the book A, it is advised to categorize the book based on its subject matter by succinctly articulating the overarching theme and content of the entire work. Please endeavor to be succinct. Kindly provide a comprehensive enumeration of the primary components, arranged in a sequential and interconnected manner. Please delineate these components in the manner you delineated the entirety of D. Elucidate the issue or issues that the author endeavors to address. The ultimate stage of reading transcends topicality, necessitating the engagement with books of similar subject matter and emboldening oneself to delve into the practice of scrutinizing and juxtaposing their contents. As you progress through these levels, you will observe yourself gradually assimilating the cerebral techniques of impression association and repetition as you go. Delving deeper into the book, specifically at the analytical and thematic levels, will facilitate the solidification of the book's impact on your memory, foster connections to previously read works, and reinforce the concepts you have acquired. This will be achieved through a methodical and intentional approach to engage with the various levels of reading. Additionally, another method for enhancing recollection of the books you have read is as follows. Ensure that you maintain comprehensive notes, making marginal annotations while proceeding. Please mark your preferred excerpts once you have completed the review. Utilize your Kindle highlights extensively, and subsequently, revisit your notes at regular intervals for the purpose of review and refreshing. The specific note-taking method employed during the review process is inconsequential, as long as a method is utilized. Strive for utmost simplicity in its completion to enhance your ability to diligently carry out the task.

RETENTION

One challenge associated with cultivating speed reading abilities is that by the time one becomes aware of the book's lack of interest, it has already been fully perused. Quote by Franklin P.

Jones, were you aware that the current holder of the title of world speed reading champion possesses the remarkable ability to comprehend and interpret a total of four thousand seven hundred words within a span of sixty seconds? This implies that an individual can effortlessly navigate lengthy novels and books within a time frame of under an hour. Nevertheless, at such a velocity, there is remarkably little knowledge and information left to acquire and retain. If one is reading Inferno or Harry Potter, it is acceptable to read swiftly as the intention is purely recreational. Nevertheless, in the pursuit of exam preparation, it is imperative to condition one's mind to exhibit curiosity and receptiveness towards knowledge acquisition in order to effectively comprehend the information within the text at hand. Reading it will not necessarily result in learning. Today, I would like to discuss the topic of memory as it relates to the act of reading. Basically retention. In fact, there exist three methods by which one can effectively retain information from reading material. It is advisable to engage in cognitive exercises such as impression Association and repetition to enhance cognitive abilities. Commencing the journey of fostering book retention can be facilitated by comprehending fundamental mechanisms by which our brain encodes and retains information. Please find below these three specific elements for consideration. First impression, secondly. Association number 3. Repetition. Suppose we consider the scenario in which you have perused Dale Carnegie's renowned literary work, titled How to Win Friends And Influence People. You were highly appreciative of the information and are eager to retain it to the best of your abilities. Allow me to provide you with instructions on how to accomplish this task. Start with impression. Kindly appreciate the written content and vividly envision an image within your imagination. Including elements such as a profound sense of magnificence and an unexpected appearance by oneself, to elevate the impact. If Dale Carnegie is elucidating his aversion towards criticism. Envision yourself being awarded the Nobel Prize for Peace and subsequently demonstrating jubilation by raising and exuberantly celebrating with the prestigious accolade. Onto the days. Another method for creating a lasting impact is by reciting a significant excerpt audibly, as some individuals may have a heightened receptivity to auditory stimuli compared to visual content. Subsequently, the following step involves establishing an association to connect the text with existing knowledge. This method is employed to great efficacy when it comes to memorization and the establishment of memory palaces. If there is a specific example from Carnegie's book that you intend to preserve. Reflect upon a past experience wherein you played a role in a particular scenario that involved the principal. Establishing connections through prior knowledge is an effective method to develop associations. And lastly repetition. With increased repetition comes heightened recollection. This can manifest through a direct process of reading a specific passage, or by employing techniques such as highlighting or transcribing it in writing. Subsequently, revisiting the aforementioned exercise and diligently honing these three facets of recall will progressively enhance your performance, ensuring that the more effort you exert, the more information you will retain.

Types Of Reading

The particular genre or category of literature being read can influence the rate at which you engage in reading. Due to the impact of environmental factors, each individual possesses a distinct neurological configuration. Since our early years in grade school, teachers have instructed us to read word by word, yet they have failed to provide guidance on how to enhance this approach or emphasize its significance.

While engaging in careful word-by-word reading, it is common for one's eyes to involuntarily regress to the preceding line or word. You may also become fixated on a single word even after having read it. These concerns impede your reading pace and impact your comprehension of the text. In a broad sense, there exist three classifications of reading. They include:

1. Subvocalization, or mental phonation, refers to the internalized articulation of each word while reading, akin to silently reading to oneself. This reading modality exhibits the lowest speed.

2. Aural reading: this entails perceiving the words you read through your sense of hearing. Relative to the process of sub vocalization, this technique exhibits greater efficiency in terms of speed.

3. Visual interpretation: in this form of interpretation, the comprehension of a word is achieved through visual perception rather than auditory perception or phonetics. This represents the most expedient form of reading and the primary subject matter of this book.

What is the rate at which speed reading is performed?

Mental readers have the capacity to peruse a maximum of 250 words within a minute. Auditory readers have the capacity to read approximately 450 words per minute, whereas visual readers exhibit the ability to read in excess of 700 words per minute.

Speed-reading has a varying range, spanning from a few hundred words per minute to approximately 1200 words per minute. In alternative scenarios, certain individuals proficient in rapid reading may exceed prescribed limits, reaching significantly accelerated rates. Howard Berg, renowned for his unparalleled reading prowess, boasts a remarkable reading velocity of 25,000 words per minute.

Moreover, there are additional classifications of speed-reading where proponents assert achieving astonishing speeds of up to 40,000 words per minute or beyond. This assertion lacks substantiated evidence, and a portion of scientists assert that it is implausible for the average human intellect to attain such velocities and comprehend them.

Influences on Your Reading Speed

There are several variables that can impact the pace at which an individual engages in the act of reading. They include:

Preferred writing style: The preferred composition style in a book holds significance as certain writers may exhibit inadequate organization in their works, while others may employ excessively technical vocabulary, thus diminishing the reader's involvement with the material. This ultimately results in decelerating the pace at which one reads and comprehends the written material.

Book genre: This aspect significantly impacts the rate at which one reads. Typically, the literary genre you engage with can have an impact on your reading pace. Take, for example, if one enjoys perusing romance literature and thereafter selects a work of non-fiction, a discernible adjustment in one's pace of reading might be observed.

Please be advised that altering book genres is not inherently incorrect; rather, it is important to acknowledge that certain genres may possess intricacies that could potentially impede the pace at which you read.

Your degree of acquaintance with the subject matter of the book. A plausible illustration in this context would be if you have previously perused approximately five books pertaining to a specific subject, subsequent readings on the same topic would prove less challenging as you would possess a level of familiarity with the underlying theories, terminology, and principles associated with said subject.

Thus, subsequent to the initial five books, you will encounter less difficulty in comprehending information or encountering frequent interruptions. Nevertheless, if you were to engage with a subject matter in which you lack proficiency, it would require a significant amount of time to assimilate the concepts, thus impeding the pace of your reading and writing.

The employed method of reading: Reading is an acquired proficiency, requiring the application of a suitable technique to achieve effectiveness. If you aspire to enhance your reading speed, you will need to employ a technique that is most suitable for you (explained subsequently in this publication). The advantage of employing reading techniques is that they do not require extensive practice before yielding favorable outcomes.

Your Focus: As previously mentioned, maintaining a high level of concentration is paramount when engaging in speed-reading activities. In order to efficiently engage in speed reading, it is imperative to uphold a high level of concentration, thereby enabling the maintenance of reading velocity while ensuring comprehension of the material.

Speed-Reading Criticisms

Certain critics of speed-reading contend that the practice thereof renders reading an arduous endeavor and diminishes the reader's level of comprehension. To a certain extent, these assertions hold validity. Nevertheless, the aforementioned effects are ephemeral.

Typically, when acquiring a novel proficiency, the initial stages can be challenging and devoid of pleasure. It requires a significant amount of time to transition from a recently acquired skill being consciously performed to becoming proficient enough to execute it with ease. When acquiring the skill of speed-reading, one is essentially undergoing a process of reacquainting oneself with the art of reading.

As an illustration, if we were to harken back to a couple of years ago, during the time when you were acquainting yourself with the art of bicycling, you experienced consecutive episodes of toppling over, struggling to maintain equilibrium, and even encountering difficulty in achieving forward momentum. During that period, it is probable that you did not derive pleasure from cycling or embarking on any journeys, since you were still in the process of acquiring the necessary skills.

This principle holds true for the practice of speed-reading and the acquisition of effective techniques therein. When acquiring the skill of speed-reading, the enjoyment is likely to intensify post-mastery rather than during the active acquisition stage. To acquire this proficiency, one must possess the virtue of patience.

With the foundational principles established, let us now proceed to explore our focal point of examination in greater depth and comprehend the techniques involved in enhancing reading speed.

Speed Reading Techniques

The gestural actions have the potential to cause harm to individuals rather than serving as a beneficial aid. By incorporating another element into your reading, you are essentially introducing an aid that may impede your progress instead of facilitating it. Moreover, the manner in which pages are turned during reading can serve as a contributing factor to slow reading speed and diminished comprehension. Furthermore, an array of advantageous strategies can be employed to enhance one's reading abilities.

• Indicating: Indicating refers to the action of utilizing a hand, finger, writing instrument, or any other implement as a means to maintain alignment with a specific line. Nevertheless, this practice is superfluous and results in the unnecessary consumption of energy. When engaging in reading, it is important to have the entirety of the page accessible to facilitate an enhanced visual experience, rather than confining oneself to reading only a single line at a time. If you are encountering difficulty in overcoming this habit, it may be necessary for you to physically restrain your hands while reading until you can engage in reading without their assistance.

This is a practice frequently endorsed by professionals in the field of accelerated reading; nonetheless, it is advisable to refrain from adopting this habit. Whenever you obscure the page, be it with your hand or a card, you are constraining your capacity to fully comprehend the written content. Engagement in any form of hand or finger movement merely serves as a source of distraction.

Cumbersome Page Navigation: Although seemingly inconsequential, extensive observations have revealed that a sluggish page turning experience significantly hampers reading effectiveness. On average, readers require approximately four seconds to proceed from one page to the next and resume their reading. This duration is equivalent to the time required for numerous proficient readers to peruse an entire page. A decrease in the speed of page turning can potentially lead to not only a deceleration in reading pace but also exert an influence on one's rate of comprehension. If the act of turning a page consumes four seconds of your time, it consequently leads to a non-negligible loss of several minutes during the process of perusing any form of written material.

In an ideal scenario, the printing of books on a continuous sheet would be desirable; however, such a method would pose challenges for the storage of books in libraries and bookstores. The author's continuum of ideas extends beyond the conclusion of each page, posing challenges in grasping a comprehensive understanding of the text, particularly when it requires a substantial four seconds to transition to the subsequent page.

A method to accelerate the turning of pages involves gently bending the spine of the book. This facilitates swift page flipping. While grasping the book firmly with both hands, apply firm and repetitive pressure to force the covers to converge at the spine.

The act of "breaking" should be performed at intervals of approximately ten to fifteen pages. The procedure induces the loosening of the binding, thereby facilitating the pages to assume a lying flat position. This alleviates the need for manually securing the pages, thereby increasing the time required for page-turning. Naturally, you are solely inclined to dismantle the spines of books within your personal possession. This procedure is typically necessary solely for paperbound books, as hardcover editions will naturally remain open.

- Skimming involves purposefully reading your material while striving for a comprehensive grasp of the chosen particulars. When engaging in skimming, it is imperative to approach the task with a clear objective in mind:

You are attempting to extract key concepts from an extensive volume of literature.

You are evaluating the possibility of omitting a section of the reading material without any adverse consequences.

To locate and thoroughly review the necessary materials.

In order to gain a comprehensive overview without requiring in-depth expertise.

"There exist various materials that are well-suited for the practice of skimming, which encompass:

⬛ Online platforms ⬛ Digital portals ⬛ Internet-based platforms ⬛ Cyber platforms ⬛ Online domains

⬛ Periodicals

Newspapers serve as a means of disseminating information.

⬛ Books of a factual nature
⬛ Instructional guides
Electronic magazines

Skimming bears resemblance to previewing, with the exception of one distinction. When engaging in skimming, you contribute additional elements to the process beyond merely perusing the initial sentence of a paragraph. When engaging in a cursory examination, it may be necessary to peruse several lines of text rather than merely a single sentence. Subsequently, you will permit your gaze to peruse the passage in search of noteworthy keywords. In addition, it is imperative for you to actively search for numerical figures, specific dates, individual names, and any other pertinent details that may catch your attention. Subsequently, proceed to peruse the final sentence within the aforementioned paragraph. Although this procedure might appear time-consuming, it can be accomplished expeditiously once you grasp its efficiency.

Scanning entails a process contrary to skimming. You consistently engage in the practice of scanning reading materials, albeit unknowingly in most instances. There exist a variety of reading materials which you shall peruse, comprising:

Conducting online research

Television schedule

• Precise subjects listed in an index or Table of Contents.

▪ Results pertaining to the athletic division.

Telephone numbers or individuals' names listed within a telephone directory.

Simultaneous employment of skimming and scanning techniques can demonstrate symbiotic effectiveness. You may briefly peruse the headlines of the newspaper, whereas you may thoroughly examine the article in search of specific details that capture your attention.

Scanning can be conducted at a high speed, reaching up to 1,500 words per minute. Due to the fact that you are commonly in search of a particular detail or fact when you are scanning, it is highly probable that you possess a strong level of comprehension regarding the information you are seeking.

Omitting: Omitting portions while reading entails skipping the complete section. When you skip at any point in your reading, then it is probably material that is unnecessary or just filler. A proficient reader demonstrates the ability to discern the appropriate moments to omit a segment. Skipping can be considered as a form of discerning reading. One may opt to completely forgo reading a section if:

The material does not contain any novel information. It encompasses no pertinent information. If one pursues a diverse array of reading materials over an extended duration, it is likely that they will encounter a considerable amount of content that can be omitted during their reading. For example, in the event that you peruse newspapers, websites, or magazines focusing on a specific subject and encounter a repetition of key facts or points, it is likely that you can forego reading certain sections of the material in their entirety. In addition, previewing and skimming facilitate the identification of sections that may be safely omitted.

Chapter 4: The Proficiencies in Navigating Diverse Formats of Text

Various kinds of documents contain information in distinct locations and diverse manners, exhibiting varying degrees of depth and scope. In order to effectively retrieve the relevant information, it is imperative to comprehend the structure and organization of the material being perused. Allow us to contemplate the most optimal tactics for addressing diverse forms of written material.

Magazines and Newspapers

Magazines often prioritize the most captivating and appealing aspects of a subject matter, as it aids in increasing their readership. Consequently, these publications tend to provide a fragmented portrayal by disregarding the 'less intriguing' elements (which may be crucial for a comprehensive understanding of the topic).

One should employ the method of perusing the tables of contents or indexes in magazines, and subsequently proceed to directly access articles of personal interest, as it proves to be the most efficient approach for acquiring information. If you discover an article to be of value, we suggest that you physically remove it and organize it within a designated folder intended for the purpose of archiving comparable information. Over time, one accumulates collections of interconnected articles that might progressively shed light on the given topic.

Newspapers typically adopt a structural organization into distinct sections. By reading a paper frequently, you can promptly discern the sections that hold value (and gather them), while identifying the sections that can be omitted entirely.

In the context of perusing online newspapers, individuals have the option to conveniently store the hyperlinks in a designated bookmark directory for future reference. Please ensure that you provide appropriate titles to your folders in order to facilitate easy retrieval of the respective content in the future. It is crucial to bear in mind that one should refrain from losing focus due to hyperlinks leading to unrelated content. The remainder of the approach remains consistent with that of perusing a physical newspaper.

Reading Individual Articles

When the reader accurately identifies the genre of an article and possesses precise knowledge of their search objectives, the process of reading is expedited and conducted with superior efficiency.

There exist three primary categories of articles that are readily accessible through both online platforms and print publications:

News articles are crafted to initially present the pivotal information before delving into its subsequent elaboration. Consequently, the primary and crucial details are presented right at the onset of said articles, with the subsequent information becoming progressively less informative as the article unfolds.

Perspective Pieces – These convey a particular viewpoint. Although these statements may exhibit some level of bias due to the author's viewpoint, the introduction and the summary sections contain the most crucial information. The central segments of these articles comprise corroborating arguments.

Feature Articles – Written to provide entertainment or background on a subject, the most important information typically lies in the body of the text.

When engaging with online articles, it is recommended to save the links using appropriate titles within designated folders. This will facilitate easier referencing of the articles in subsequent instances. On certain occasions, designating the title of the folder as the name of the website or publication can serve the same purpose, allowing for the organization of different links that have been sourced from a specific website.

Occasionally, readers may encounter challenges when perusing lengthy or intricate articles online. It is important to bear in mind that there exist electronic documents or articles that were not initially intended for online reading. If you find that your reading skills are being impeded by reading online documents, you may consider attempting to print them out.

••Chapter 3: Advantages of Rapid Reading

In addition to the evident advantage of being able to read through numerous books efficiently and potentially maintaining academic success while pursuing a degree, speed reading offers various other merits that specifically cater to college and graduate students. Nevertheless, this is not the sole rationale behind the advantages that speed reading can bestow upon any individual committed to effectively incorporating it into their routine.

Enhanced memory is one of the advantages associated with the practice of speed reading. The human mind can be likened to a muscle, and numerous justifications exist for individuals' pursuit of cognitive exercises. Similar to the manner in which we strengthen our biceps through rigorous and extended training, fostering our mental acuity through stimulating activities yields comparable fortification. When engaged in speed reading, the mind is not only compelled to assimilate information at an accelerated pace, but it also undergoes the cognitive demand of effectively sifting and retaining the information to a greater degree compared to its accustomed level of functioning. Consider speed reading as the act of incorporating an additional 5-pound weight plate to both ends of your squat rack. Initially, the task appears intimidating, causing one's legs to tremble in supplication. However, with consistent practice, the 5-pound plate gradually becomes a 10-pound plate, leading to the strengthening of both the mind and the neural pathways associated with information retrieval and retention in long-term memory banks.

An additional notable advantage lies in the concept of enhanced concentration. A significant number of individuals have the capacity to read at a rate of 200 words per minute. This pertains to the typical reading pace, which equates to approximately three or four words per second. However, it is notable that a nearly equivalent proportion of individuals possess the ability to comprehend written material at a rate of up to 300 words per minute, demonstrating a considerable improvement of 50% compared to the aforementioned group. What is the reason behind the existence of such a substantial disparity?

There are two factors contributing to this situation: firstly, the conventional approach employed in teaching children to read proves to be inefficient; secondly, there is a notable lack of concentration. If an individual is unable to maintain their focus on the text at hand, it is highly unlikely that they will be able to initiate a proper understanding of the material presented before them. A deficiency in concentration leads to mental distraction, resulting in a regression in reading skills. This is the location in which you devoted a greater amount of time in pursuit of the most recent memory prior to discovering yourself several sentences, or perhaps an entire page, behind your actual position subsequent to the moment your concentration was relinquished. Speed reading enhances concentration by incorporating memory retention exercises into the methodologies, thereby cultivating mastery of the skill. These retention exercises focus on a particular facet of speed reading and diligently work on it, crafting exercises that individuals can employ to enhance their memory retention and retrieval.

Is it an aspect that it specifically focuses on? An individual's capacity for concentration.

Speed reading also cultivates a greater sense of self-assurance in the individual honing their proficiency in this skill. When the acquisition of any new skill becomes achievable for individuals, it instills a sense of pride upon successful attainment. A college graduate who confidently displays their diploma is filled with a sense of pride and basking in the glory of their accomplishments. An individual who successfully completes the acquisition of a language, thereby attaining proficiency, emerges from the examination chamber and wholeheartedly engages in the local culture, exuding delight as they engage in effortless and uninhibited conversations with the indigenous population. An aspiring thespian secures his inaugural substantial acting opportunity in a motion picture that holds the promise of propelling him towards the professional trajectory he has long yearned for.

In each of these situations, an individual experiences a deep sense of pride upon considering the prospect of achieving something they have dedicated their entire lives to working towards and honing their skills for." Although individuals may not have dedicated their entire lives to practicing speed reading, the capacity to embark on a new skill and persevere until achieving expertise is a source of immense pride for everyone in our global community. Therefore, it is logical to conclude that attaining mastery in the technique of speed reading can foster considerable levels of self-assurance. This is not solely due to successfully acquiring a new skill, but also because of the vast array of opportunities and knowledge that speed reading can now unlock.

Furthermore, the practice of speed reading enhances logical thinking. Reading is a cognitive activity that stimulates the brain and prompts the utilization of techniques to enhance information retention and recall. Consequently, the brain undergoes adaptation, similar to how other organs in the body respond to changing circumstances. It discovers increasingly effective methods to establish, retain, and retrieve information, fostering the expansion of neural networks that can enhance an individual's cognitive capacity. When subjected to an unfamiliar environment, one might experience a sense of discomfort as their body adjusts. Nevertheless, it is unlikely that your body will undergo liquefaction due to the prevailing temperature of 105 degrees Fahrenheit coupled with 80% humidity, although you might experience the sensation of such an occurrence. Your physiological system demonstrates remarkable resilience as it adjusts to the prevailing circumstances, sustaining life and flourishing notwithstanding the altered conditions.

It endeavors to enhance its operational effectiveness, and your brain is no exception.

Through the adoption of speed reading and the diligent refinement of this skill, the cerebral faculties are actively engaged, compelled to adapt and match the demands imposed upon them. It exhibits adaptability akin to that of the human body, optimizing its processes to accelerate the input, retention, and recall of information. This phenomenon will lead to enhanced cognitive abilities in individuals as the intricate network of neural pathways expands, facilitating optimal transmission of electrical impulses within the brain.

Enhancing one's speed reading abilities can be likened to constructing an efficient network of neural pathways within the mind. This neural network serves as a direct route, akin to a well-constructed highway, enabling electrical signals to swiftly traverse and reach their destination notably earlier, as opposed to traversing the lengthier and less efficient alternate routes.

In addition to those advantages, speed reading further contributes to a heightened state of emotional well-being. Engaging in the act of reading can be an immensely calming pursuit for individuals who take pleasure in this literary undertaking. It possesses the ability to alleviate stress by diverting attention away from daily concerns and cognitive distractions that typically obscure mental clarity. Frequently, the emotions and internal narratives that manifest within the realm of our thoughts tend to be predominantly negative, thereby diminishing our self-worth in a distinct manner. When one possesses the capacity to read at a faster pace, one is able to engross oneself more deeply in the information being read. Regardless of whether it is for academic purposes or personal enjoyment, your priority will lie in thoroughly immersing yourself in the text at hand. This will enable you to effectively detach from any potential stressors or intrusive thoughts that may otherwise impede your mental clarity.

Indeed, there exists a designation for this particular concept. This practice is referred to as "active meditation." It involves attaining a meditative state through engaging in an activity that sufficiently absorbs one's conscious thought, effectively excluding all other distractions and detaching them from one's conscious mind. This state possesses the capacity to induce a profound sense of relaxation akin to that of a conventional meditative state. It also serves to mitigate the excessive release of cortisol experienced by a compromised immune system affected by chronic stress, thereby fostering an enhancement in one's holistic well-being. Additionally, it grants the body an opportunity to initiate physical healing, counteracting the detrimental impact of emotional stress on the body.

Nevertheless, the concept of thought leadership stands out as the foremost advantage that can be derived from the practice of speed reading. Put simply, the greater your comprehension and knowledge, the more capacity you possess to revolutionize and reshape the world in your presence. Developing the proficiency of rapid reading entails more than just increased efficiency in processing academic materials, providing additional leisure time. It also empowers individuals to comprehend complex literary works, scholarly articles, and digital content that may otherwise pose challenges or induce confusion. Thought leaders demonstrate exceptional skill in fostering intellectual hybridization—an intellectual process characterized by the merging of seemingly incongruous ideas and concepts, resulting in novel, invigorating, and progressive approaches that not only enrich their own understanding but also benefit society at large.

It aligns with the concept of enhanced cognitive abilities, encompassing the aptitude to reframe problems and discern logical relationships between two pieces of information or types of data that were initially unapparent. Individuals within the sphere of thought leadership and industry are not mere problem solvers; rather, they assume the roles of developers, enhancers, implementers, and entrepreneurs.

Speed reading can not only boost an individual's inner confidence and self-belief but also significantly influence their perception, reasoning, interpretation, and ultimately mastery of the world around them. Speed reading offers a gateway to a myriad of unexplored possibilities, encompassing fresh avenues for professional growth, unique avenues to cultivate enduring connections, and even unprecedented opportunities to advance one's career trajectory within their chosen vocation.

Nevertheless, the effectiveness of speed reading depends on one's ability to elevate information retention and recall. As such, aspiring speed readers can employ various techniques and strategies to continually improve this skill, regardless of their current level of proficiency in speed reading.

Mitigate Sub-Vocalization And Minimize Your Eye Movements

Furthermore, sub-vocalization and the occurrence of multiple eye fixations during the act of reading are two additional widely observed practices that have the effect of decreasing one's reading speed.

To enhance your reading speed within a one-hour time frame, it is advisable to exercise control over the tendency to engage in sub-vocalization during reading, and also minimize the frequency of eye fixations. "We will now proceed to discuss the methodology for accomplishing both tasks:

Strategies for Minimizing Ocular Fixation

As we peruse the text, our visual gaze transitions between various focal points. We classify this phenomenon as 'saccading', and the proper pronunciation is su-kawd-ing. Each location that your gaze rests upon while engaging in reading is considered an 'impression' or a 'fixation.' By pausing at various points throughout the text, you experience multiple fixations, indicating frequent pauses during the reading process.

Frequently pausing hinders the continuity of your reading experience. Additionally, it leads to the tendency of regressing to previous words or overly fixating on a singular point, rather than progressing smoothly through the entirety of the content. Individuals with a sluggish reading pace often exhibit multiple eye fixations, a significant factor influencing their reduced reading speed.

Having multiple fixations implies that you frequently interrupt your reading and grasp only a limited segment of words before proceeding. To enhance your reading velocity, it is imperative that you minimize the frequency of your eye pauses and adopt a seamless reading rhythm.

In order to accomplish this, initially ascertain if you experience multiple eye fixations during the act of reading. Adopt the practice of partially occluding one eye prior to reading, and proceed to read with the unobstructed eye, while maintaining a single line of focus. Should you perceive distinct, individual movements while perusing the entire sentence, it signifies the presence of multiple instances of eye fixations.

Presented herein are various supplementary strategies that can be employed to minimize eye fixations and enhance reading speed within a duration of less than one hour.

One effective technique that can be employed to reduce eye fixations is to engage in reading with the assistance of a pointer. Gently trace a pencil, pen, or even your finger across the sentences as you read, thereby maintaining a steady progression of your reading.

Additionally, opt to read a collection of words as opposed to reading individual words sequentially. Refrain from pausing to ponder the significance of each word encountered during the reading process. Conversely, consider reading a cluster of 4 to 7 words collectively in order to efficiently progress through a sentence.

Take note of your visual fixation points and actively strive to decrease them by 2 to 3 fixations on each occasion. If your current number of fixations amounts to ten, endeavor to peruse the subsequent sentence or paragraph with a reduced count of seven fixations. Gradually, endeavor to further reduce this count to five fixations, and subsequently down to three fixations per page.

Furthermore, enhance your ability to perceive stimuli in your visual periphery to effectively minimize the frequency of focal points required during the process of reading. By employing the technique of using the pointer on multiple occasions, you will notice an enhancement in your peripheral vision. A more effective approach to attain the desired outcome would be to increase the speed of the pointer/tracker with each iteration. After approximately 5 to 6 endeavors, you will expedite the movement of the tracker across the paragraph, thereby augmenting the swiftness of your eyes and enhancing their ability to assimilate multiple words simultaneously.

Assume an upright posture in the chair and gently shut your eyes. Engage one of your eyes and direct your gaze towards an object situated at a distance of 10 feet, allowing your attention to linger for a few moments. Following this, redirect your visual focus towards an object positioned at a distance of 2 feet. Please perform the same action on your other eye. Engage in this exercise five instances while utilizing both eyes, followed by perusing a written piece. One will observe a heightened efficiency in the movement of one's eyes across the page, resulting in the assimilation of a greater amount of information with reduced instances of fixation.

Please keep in mind the importance of maintaining a composed and patient demeanor while engaging in these exercises. By doing so, the resulting benefits will significantly manifest within a timeframe of 30 to 40 minutes.

Furthermore, aside from altering the pattern of your eye movements, it is imperative to develop the ability to overcome sub-vocalization, as this prevalent habit is another contributing factor to your reading speed deficiency.

Strategies for Mitigating Sub-vocalization

Sub-vocalization pertains to the internal articulation of words while reading. Individuals who engage in sub-vocalization exhibit a reading pace within the range of 250 to 300 words per minute, a rate that is considered to be considerably sluggish. One's cognitive faculties, including visual and mental processing, do not achieve heightened efficiency when engaged in a constant internal dialogue. When engaging in sub-vocalization, a simultaneous allocation of attention by the eyes and brain is necessary. Firstly, attention is directed towards the words being read, followed by the mental focus on the words being silently pronounced.

Maintain diligent focus on the movements of your mouth and lips whilst engaging in sentence-reading activities, and should they be in motion during the process, it signifies the presence of sub-vocalization. To enhance your reading speed, refrain from engaging in sub-vocalization. If you dedicate 20 minutes of your time to practicing the aforementioned techniques, your reading speed will exhibit a notable improvement of no less than 50 to 60 words per minute.

When perusing written material, proceed to enumerate gradually from one to ten. At the outset, this may lead to a decrease in your speed, however, with approximately ten repetitions, you will observe an improvement in your reading velocity. When mentally tallying, the opportunity to engage in sub-vocalization, thereby enhancing text concentration and reading speed, is precluded.

While engaged in the act of reading, consider the practice of chewing gum as a means to occupy and engage your oral faculties. Inevitably, when engaging in oral activity, it is probable that one would cease sub-vocalization, subsequently resulting in an accelerated pace of reading. In the event of hunger, one may also choose to consume nuts or alternative snack options. At times, the sensation of hunger might lead to sub-vocalization. It is paramount to suppress your hunger in order to prevent any potential distraction from your reading.

It is recommended to consistently utilize a pointer or tracker while reading, particularly during the initial weeks of practicing to enhance reading speed. By employing a tracker for a duration of 30 minutes, a discernible observation can be made in terms of increased reading speed and a reduced frequency of sub-vocalization.

Please remain mindful of your tendency to engage in sub-vocalization, and should you observe the movement of your lips or the repetitive mental recitation of words, kindly pause momentarily from your reading. During this intermission, engage in deep respiration, remind yourself of the written material at hand, and proceed by actively perusing it. Please exercise mindfulness and attentiveness towards your thoughts. Whenever you engage in sub-vocalization, kindly take a moment to pause, contemplate, take a deep breath, and then resume your reading. Performing this action repetitively, approximately 4 to 5 instances, will facilitate the eradication of mental clutter, recalibrate your attention towards the textual content, and enhance your reading speed by minimizing subvocalization.

To mitigate sub-vocalization, consider utilizing the AccelaReader application. Alternatively, one may utilize it on the internet by visiting the website https://accelareader.com/. Merely replicate and insert the text that you wish to peruse within the designated text field. Subsequently, configure the preferred reading pace and commence the application. If your aim is to achieve a reading speed of 400 words per minute within an hour, and your current reading speed stands at 350 words per minute, it is advisable to establish the target reading speed as 400. Each day, establish a fresh objective that exceeds your previous day's speed by an increment of 20 to 50 words. The text entered into the text box will exhibit a blinking effect at the predetermined rate, thus enhancing reading speed and facilitating swift progression through the text. The more rapidly you engage in reading, the lower your tendency to sub-vocalize will be.

Utilize these strategies and establish concise 5 to 10-minute objectives to enhance your efficiency through brief intervals of 5 minutes. For example, let us hypothesize that you possess a total of ten fixations, and exhibit a tendency to engage in sub-vocalization during the process of reading. In this particular scenario, it is recommended to utilize the initial 5 to 10 minutes as an opportunity to decrease your fixations from a severity of 10 to 7, while also making the adjustment to sub-vocalizing once every three sentences instead of engaging in sub-vocalization after every sentence. By adhering to this strategy, you will notice a notable enhancement in your reading speed and comprehension level with each successive 5 to 10-minute interval, ultimately resulting in significant improvement by the conclusion of the hour.

By solely adhering to these suggestions, you will enhance and expedite your reading speed. The upcoming chapter will present you with supplementary techniques that can be utilized to enhance your speed even more effectively.

www.ingramcontent.com/pod-product-compliance
Lightning Source LLC
Chambersburg PA
CBHW050247120526
44590CB00016B/2247